Dedicating this book to loved ones near and far, best wishes.

... "of our times"

Forty dreams in poetry

david stephens

authorHOUSE®

AuthorHouse™ UK
1663 Liberty Drive
Bloomington, IN 47403 USA
www.authorhouse.co.uk
Phone: 0800.197.4150

© 2012 david stephens. All rights reserved.

No part of this book may be reproduced, stored in a retrieval system, or transmitted by any means without the written permission of the author.

Published by AuthorHouse 12/10/2018

ISBN: 978-1-4678-9749-5 (sc)
ISBN: 978-1-4678-9748-8 (e)

Print information available on the last page.

Any people depicted in stock imagery provided by Getty Images are models, and such images are being used for illustrative purposes only.
Certain stock imagery © Getty Images.

This book is printed on acid-free paper.

Because of the dynamic nature of the Internet, any web addresses or links contained in this book may have changed since publication and may no longer be valid. The views expressed in this work are solely those of the author and do not necessarily reflect the views of the publisher, and the publisher hereby disclaims any responsibility for them.

CONTENTS

1. A smile 1
2. Fashion 3
3. To dreams 5
4. Act A Certain Way 7
5. Player 9
6. Ignite 11
7. Lonely thoughts 13
8. Meet clarity 15
9. Coffee Culture 17
10. Fight 19
11. Funny? 21
12. Coffee House 23
13. Paths 25
14. Faith 27
15. To the sounds of music 29
16. Mr. black crow 31
17. Gamer 33
18. Gunny * 35
19. To impulses 37
20. Artist 39
21. Moments 41
22. Orchid * 43
23. Cars 45
24. Subway 47
25. Presence of mind + body = hero 49
26. Photo me 51
27. Incinerator 53
28. Trillion dollar lawyer 55
29. Of our times 57
30. HOPE 59
31. WW11 Boy 61
32. The understatesman 63
33. Am I alive? 65
34. With you in mind 67
35. Year of the activist 69
36. Season greetings! 71
37. Show me your hand 73
38. To concepts 75
39. Gallery art: objects of desire 77
40. To catch a romantic 79

"In true love, for a while."

A SMILE

A smile

Is a smile.

In true love

For a while.

Eyes light up

Worlds go by

We'll smile,

To a smile.

"To be a hero, for size zero!"

FASHION

Its skin deep

I won't eat!

To be a Hero

For size Zero!

Windows look

They call me in!

Soo this season!

Is my reason!

Exit and smile,

The same style?

As me, ah I see.

"To wish for, to kiss for."

TO DREAMS

To **live** for

To **die** for

To **stay** for

To **play** for

To **wish** for

To **kiss** for.

"Congratulate the applause, given to thee."

ACT A CERTAIN WAY

It all starts in the isles

As we swiftly dance by.

Gratefully we look on

At museum's Art

Without value

To our hearts

We admire whose

Displayed on TV

Congratulate

The applause

Given to thee.

We carousel

The dance floor.

Despise our rivals

We ignore.

A familiar act

I am sure.

"Go see damsels fly."

PLAYER

Go see the rain

Go feel the pain

For reason's sake

Not just to brake

Go hear the cries

Go see damsels fly

Go slow down time

Smell opened bread

Hear what was said

Go right your demons

Don't just feed them.

Go on, lift your brow!

No need to follow now.

"Don't let your senses be dictated"

IGNITE

Your last-gasp-of breath

That free-flowing-dress

Your slight-of-touch

Ignites all-too-much.

I know all-to-impress.

*I will never become **sedated.***

*Don't let your senses be **dictated**.*

*Just remember, you're the **greatest**.*

"Look through reason, not your cross-hair."

LONELY THOUGHTS

The dark desert shimmers tonight.

I see there, my frozen-breath-alight.

A voice side-winds through the air.

"Am I the gunfire you hear over there?

Look through reason, not your cross-hair.

Come, let truthful words hold resonance.

Believe in one another, not miss-held ones.

Don't be another war-remembrance-son.

And words be more powerful, than the gun"

"Tell inertia, I'm heading her way."

MEET CLARITY

Pull shyness

From the well.

Let truthfulness tell.

No need to agitate sand,

The foretold is as planned.

Leave impulse to go and play,

Tell inertia, I'm heading her way.

Give up, relating the unrelated dear.

Trying to be clear, trying to be sincere

Step back, listen, it's all in front to absorb.

Looking at puzzles that are hidden, no more.

"An espresso entails, enjoyed, as I inhale."

COFFEE CULTURE

Romantic gestures

On suggestive walls

Feeling like Naples.

Timeless classics

Perfected cultures.

Deep, dark secrets

An espresso entails.

Enjoyed, as I inhale.

"For humanity, for humility."

FIGHT

The haze

The ways

The smiles

For miles

For chance

For romance

For kindness

For blindness

For cruelties

For humanity

For humility

For love.

"A simple juggle suffice?"

FUNNY?

I wonder what is funny.

Is it ok, just to laugh?

Do I need to tickle first?

A simple juggle suffice?

A chuckle, would be nice?

Poor beans into my bath?

Laugh when the TV laughs?

Do I need complexity too?

Is it ok....just to laugh?

For you, to laugh along too.

"Looking in, looking out."

COFFEE HOUSE

Retrospective house

Than a coffee house.

Looking on in, looking out.

"Yee who walks the path of faith."

PATHS

Yee who walks the path of faith

Wondering on the line it takes.

The path's never clear my dear

But walk forth, have no fear.

Enjoy in chances it creates

Enjoy in mistakes you make.

Did you reach your destiny?

Is it how you believed it to be?

Try not to be, but see, the best.

Drive in harmony, with your quest.

"Philosophers of such."

FAITH

In god they trust.

Philosophers of such.

Were such of legends?

Called from the skies!

From an idyllic place.

The word of the cloth.

World contradictions

Witches, sorcerers.

And the magicians.

Where the world

Was a flat plane.

Dragon's slayed.

As true, as

Me, & you.

"To colors it creates."

TO THE SOUNDS OF MUSIC

To symphonies I chose

To emotions it evokes

To pulses it generates

To colors it creates

To networks it makes

To places it may take.

"Oh death's shadow, Mr. Black Crow."

MR. BLACK CROW

Mr. Black Crow

Oh how we know

You look through

Our gaze, it's true.

For I wasn't fooled

Your use many tools.

Oh death's shadow

Mr. Black Crow.

"Colors gladly pull my trigger."

GAMER

Pitch black.
Locked away.
Let's go back.
Feel me here
The other side
Of the sphere.
In my sights
Lights flicker
Colors gladly
Pull my trigger.
Eyes like dots.
I should stop.
Perspire badly
Down my brow.
Six hours how.
Hear me now
Is it the same?
The real world?
Like us here, in
The underworld.

"Hollow barrel…of terror!"

GUNNY *

The Gun era!

Introduces...

To you...

The hollow

Barrel...

Of terror!

No remorse

In a killer.

"To passions it takes."

TO IMPULSES

To dreams I make

To passions it takes

To glimmer-night

To birds at flight

To love at stake

To fear I hate.

"Knock back-a-drink-to-renaissance."

ARTIST

An Artist, an easy word to say

Tears, sweat, resolve are first laid.

Smell the oils, and catch the joys.

Rekindle my emotional turmoil's.

Color's flowing from a white canvas.

Playing my favorite melodic chants.

Knock back-a-drink-to-renaissance

Share a dance, a faraway chance.

Just reflect, refine and so preserve.

Transcendence through the world.

An unspoken language I observed.

"Streets paved with fun."

MOMENTS

Play with a rising sun

Streets paved with fun

Moments, wait for none.

"Her shadowy remains still lay."

ORCHID *

Monday laying there in the road

An Orchid, so vibrant and pure.

Tuesday, lying beside her assured

A brightly coloured bottle top.

Wednesday, I road past and saw

Her shadowy remains still lay.

Lying there beside her still

A brightly colored bottle top!

"In eighties we trust."

CARS

Is it more reflections?

Than the perfections.

In eighties we trust!

Its robotic forms.

Through decades

To the present day.

Our cold hearted toys

Move around and play

Past roads and junctions

Does beauty follow function?

"Eyes face front!"

SUBWAY

Catch the tube!

Quick must rush!

Do I need lube?

To fit in that sub

Sudden silence.

Eyes face front!

He just looked!

Read the book!

Try the frown!

Or, ponder?

I did wonder,

Why I'm under.

"Realized into reality."

PRESENCE OF MIND + BODY = HERO

Free from ill gains.

From mind's chains.

Realized into reality.

"A shot for eternity? Unreal."

PHOTO ME

Capturing time for real.

A shot for eternity? Unreal!

You can freeze-frame play?

I'll capture my own life today!

Fools behind a tool, so uncool.

"Play that last-chance-song o' mine."

INCINERATOR

I am not looking for re-incarnation,

I want to just lie here quietly, alone.

Bring heat to these weary old bones

Warm me up, for the very last time.

Play that last-chance-song o' mine.

Enjoy all of that food, and the wine.

While I hear the song fade, I smile.

"Mind-tapping the streets."

TRILLION DOLLAR LAWYER

Mind-tapping the streets.

A hero, villain or saint?

A night crawler in daily life.

Words that seem oh-so-quaint.

Justice served, no matter the side.

A bond in society, in humanity?

From manic-child-killers-eyes.

Iron veil of misdirection.

The law, at his disposal.

A hero, villain or saint?

A trillion dollar lawyer.

"Travelling so far, but in reverse."

OF OUR TIMES

Travelling so far, but in reverse.
Far away, the promised land
Where we go, hand in hand.
Memories hark of a time before.
Fix-framed-idyllic scenes we saw.
Playing all day, a summer's day!
Look be yonder! We are fonder?
Modern times, is all our crimes.
Familiarities, held our content?
For what we are, all so hell bent.

"To drive thirst, in the glimmer-light"

HOPE

To drive thirst

In the glimmer-light

Through tunnels first

The soul thou fight.

"My heart, devoted now to pounding."

WW11 BOY

The silver screen-age.
My country needs me!
Pack up my troubles!
Soon to get my belle!
Alter my birthdate as well.
Front line, I hear it's D-day
Smell of hemp, rattle of rations
Stiff upper lip, we charge today!
My head brushes their shoulders
My heart, devoted now to pounding.
I must stick these socks to those tanks!
Disappointing looks, no need to thank!
Ouch! A quick sharp scratch on my head
My loose tin hat, now pushed to one side.
Now what is this, running down my face!
Things seem quieter now, slower in pace.
Smells seem intense, bag cushions my fall
I see legs running away, I try to grasp.
Eyes closing now, as I play games of war,
I see those patriotic posters, once more.
I am trampled on, I give out my last sigh.
Mum kisses my forehead, goodbye

"He brought the chemistry."

THE UNDERSTATESMAN

A chain of distractions

Oh, our child-like minds.

Lost to darker thoughts

Rushing into submission.

He brought the chemistry

I brought my wildcard ticket!

Flicking through frequencies.

Enter the under statesman

Oh-so quietly assured.

Now the new statesman

Innocent minded in life

Courageous in his career.

"I love hard, I'll die hard."

AM I ALIVE?

I cry hard

I play hard

I hate hard

I fall hard

I love hard

I'll die hard.

"Act aloof-like, future-proof."

WITH YOU IN MIND

New toys, new spec!

New Tech, let's check!

Grab them color-candies!

The linear or the veneers

Aesthetics or synthetics?

Are any of these sincere?

These cold dis-associations

I'll pretend I didn't know

That I was the first to grow.

Act aloof-like, future-proof.

Receptiveness, their goal?

Is our love for money, all?

Just a materialistic tool.

"Embodying a catalyst of expressions."

YEAR OF THE ACTIVIST

One thousand lights hit me.

Media serves an endless pain.

Sign of the times, a world view?

Imagination, capturing a nation.

Humoring the movement, I sigh.

Enclosed actions, imposed reactions.

Embodying a catalyst of expressions.

Repressed borders, absorbed no more.

Empathy surges through me, and & out.

"Emptiness and envy will soon be restored."

SEASON GREETINGS!

Commercialism, bringing communities closer!

Indulge in new gifts, one won't feel left out!

I hear it's the season to be jolly, let's shout!

Lights and sound, euphorically fill the void!

And of those renewed vigor's of January 1ST

Do not worry with any of those out bursts.

Emptiness and envy will soon be restored.

"Or spin me in a trance"

SHOW ME YOUR HAND

Show me your hand

Not just your plans

Your shimmer light

Your sparkling plight

Your stories-of-old

Always to be-told.

Not to make me dance

Or spin me in a trance

Or even for romance

Its ok dear, just be clear.

Just show me your hand.

Grow old and be grand.

"To music, to new-hip"

TO CONCEPTS

To **cultivate**

To **generate**

To **energize**

To **realize**

To **cinemas**

To **theatres**

To **music**

To **new-hip**

To **tune-in**

To **reason**

To **believe-in**

To **persevere**

To **fresh air**

To **touching**

To **loving.**

"Held, by a confectioner's tale."

GALLERY ART: OBJECTS OF DESIRE

Brightly-lit talents of this world

Held, by a confectioner's tale.

All colours, shapes and vases.

For low, middle or even classes?

Wondering, whom will it fool?

Do low dimly-lit souls deserve?

Introverts, on extroverts stools.

Is it wizardry or mere psychology?

To look up, look down or just around.

"To breath-calm-by-chance."

TO CATCH A ROMANTIC

To feel a-passing-glance.

To breathe-calm-by-chance.

To have a great story to tell.

To dance uncontrollably well.

To let rays radiate a room.

To let rivers flow through.

To let your pulses run true.

Let cupid take the leading role.

As innocence falls in love again.

Dedicating this book to loved ones near and far, best wishes.